A BRIEF INTRODUCTION TO HINDUISM

(Scriptures, Deities, Prayers, Mantras, Meditation Techniques, Yoga Karma, Hindu Concept of Creation, Nature & Science)

A BRIEF INTRODUCTION TO HINDUISM

(Scriptures, Deities, Prayers, Mantras, Meditation Techniques, Yoga Karma, Hindu Concept of Creation, Nature & Science)

Kandiah Sivaloganathan

ZORBA BOOKS

ZORBA BOOKS

Published in India by Zorba Books, 2017

Website: www.zorbabooks.com
Email: info@zorbabooks.com

Copyright © Kandiah Sivaloganathanl

ISBN Print Book - 978-93-86407-43-6
ISBN eBook - 978-93-86407-44-3

Zorba Books Pvt. Ltd.(opc)
Gurgaon, INDIA

Printed in India

A Brief Introduction
to the Ancient Religion
of
Hinduism

Dedicated

To

Bhagawan Sri Sathya Sai Baba

&

Saints

"No religion on earth preaches the dignity of humanity in such a lofty strain as Hinduism."

—*Swami Vivekananda*

PREFACE

In this modern world dominated by science and technology, people are disillusioned with the concept of religion. Today's youth in particular, with their inquiring mind, find it difficult to believe in the concept of religion when they can't see any tangible benefit from following a particular faith. They seek empirical evidence about the existence of an ultimate power called God. In school, students are taught to question and make enquiries before they accept anything. Therefore it becomes difficult for them to understand the language of religion based on a belief system.

Prophets in most religions, the enlightened ones like Buddha, Jesus Christ and Mohammad have preached their own experience of their enlightenment, vision, in their own language. Their language itself cannot be precise and provide the real experience of the prophets. This is similar to describing the smell of the flower one experienced to another person who has not. To experience it, one should smell the flower and not listen to another person's description of it.   In religious talks, the followers of the prophets and religious scholars amplify the prophets' teachings and even go a bit further emphasising that this is the best path not only to their followers but also to all humanity to reach heaven or God. Preaching in this manner is done with the best of intentions, but it immediately sets up a fence around each religion and creates conflict between them as to which is the best path to follow. This has even resulted in a number of wars including the present conflicts in the Middle East.   It is therefore understandable why today's youth is indifferent to religious teachings.

Most of the younger generations get a very brief understanding of their religion just by observing the religious practices of their parents, relatives and friends. In some cases, even that doesn't exist due to the apathy of their relatives towards religion.

In school, too, there's no introduction to religion, particularly in state schools where students from different backgrounds attend, so as to not to offend any particular section of parents.

Unlike in the olden days, very few, including parents, have the time or take the time, to read religious texts to get an understanding of their faith. This is particularly so with Hinduism, which does not have a holy book, like the Bible for Christians or the Quran for Muslims.

Hindu scriptures, from the Vedas, are without beginning and without an end as these are an accumulation of treasures of spiritual laws discovered at different times. Spiritual law is the relationship between individual spirits and the soul, and these laws were there even before they were discovered and will remain so even when we forget them. This is just like the laws of gravity that existed before it was discovered and continue to exist.

To understand Hinduism one needs to study the various scriptures from the Vedas to the Upanishads to the *Mahabharata* and the *Ramayana*. The Agamas are also Hindu texts, which govern the present practice of Hinduism. The *Bhagavad Gita*, which is considered as the equivalent of the Bible to Hindus, is part of the *Mahabharata,* the great epic. To read and understand these scriptures is a big undertaking for the busy individual in this day and age.

This book is an effort to provide a very brief background for the introduction to Hinduism and some simple everyday religious rituals of a Hindu householder. I hope this will kindle interest in the readers and thus encourage them to read some of the scriptures and refine their knowledge of Hinduism.

I render my grateful thanks to my friend Paul Ward–Harvey BA, LLM, for meticulously editing the manuscript. I also thank my son, Lavan, for formatting and proofreading the text.

Kandiah Sivaloganathan
Sydney, Australia

CONTENTS

1
BASIC SCRIPTURES

Hinduism is one of the oldest religions in the world with around 900 million followers. What sets apart Hinduism from other world religions is the fact that it has no single founder, no sole scripture or no common set of teachings. For these reasons, many scholars refer to it as 'a way of life'. In a gist, Hinduism is a study of the spirit and how everything came to be.

Hinduism is also –known as 'Sanatana Dharma' — the eternal way or the eternal order beyond human origins.

Several ancient scriptures provide the foundation for the Hindu religion and here is a look at some of the main texts and their teachings:

1.1 The Vedas and the Upanishads

The Vedas and the Upanishads are broadly considered as the ancient Hindu scriptures. Vedas means knowledge. Vedas is a large body of texts formulated by rishis, seers, saints and sages thousands of years ago in India. Over the years, this knowledge, made available by the rishis, concerning the Eternal Principal, was passed on from one generation to another through word of mouth and eventually made available in the written form. This written form of the knowledge of the Eternal Principal is known as *the Vedas*. The original spoken literatures are known as *Shruti* (heard).

There are four main Vedas: Rig Veda, Sama Veda, Yajur Veda and Atharva Veda.

Rig Veda is the knowledge of the hymns and songs of the rishis.

Sama Veda is a liturgical collection of the melodies for chanting and giving meaning to the words in the Rig Veda.

Yajur Veda is also a liturgical collection and meets the demands of the ceremonial religion.

Atharva Veda is different from the above three and it contains hymns that are more diverse and consists of spells and charms present at that time.

There are also several others that cover all the aspects of human endeavours including the arts and sciences.

The Upanishads are a collection of texts that contain some of the central philosophical concepts of Hinduism. The term Upanishad denotes the study and practice of the inner truth. '*Upa*' means the process of studying with '*Nishta*' or steadfastness; 'Shad' means the attainment of Ultimate Reality. The Upanishads describe the various stages of realisation of one's basic reality. They point out not only the duties and obligations one has to bear, but also the actions to be carried out and those to be avoided. The Upanishads are collectively called the *Vedanta*.

1.2 The Agamas

In addition to the Vedas, the Agamas are another type of ancient Hindu scriptures that govern the present-day practice of Hinduism. The Agamas literally mean traditions, "that which comes down". The Agamas provide practical and experimental concepts of Hindu religious beliefs and practice. These texts consist of three groups: Shaivism (related to Siva), Vaishnavism (related to Vishnu) and Shaktism (related to Devi). The Indonesian Balinese Hindus have their own Agamas known as the Agama Bali.

The Agamas are more voluminous than the Vedas but they are not known to most as they are written entirely in the Grantha script (Appendix A) and prevail mostly in southern India. The Grantha script is an old Tamil script. The Malayalam and Sinhala alphabets are the direct descendants of Grantha. Only a few Agama texts have been translated into English and French. The non-availability of Agama texts in English and other languages has led to the spread of distorted versions of Hinduism among the westerners and modern Hindus. The Agama traditions comprise approximately two third of the Hindu heritage.

The Hindu view normally presented is Vedic and Sanskrit-centred, which is not a true representation of the present-day practise of Hinduism. In the Vedic form of worship, with the fire ritual (*homa*), there is no physical representation of the deity, but where worship was necessary, visual fire represented all the gods. In the Agama rites, the deity is worshiped and represented by some visible emblem in the form of a statue, picture or a lingam. The lingam is not a *murti* but it is a sign, mark and emblem of the supreme.

Today Hinduism all over the world, and in particular in the subcontinent of India, is based on the Agamas and not the Vedic as Swami Vivekananda too has observed. The Agama scriptures cover cosmology, philosophical doctrines, meditation, yoga, mantras, temple construction, deity worship and worship in temples and homes, alter worship, temple ceremonies, and life-to-death sacraments. That is what Hinduism is all about. However, in today's practice of Hinduism, the Vedas provide the mantras, the literature (bhakti literature) and hymns to be sung in temples and homes.

In the Vedic religion, the specialists are Brahmins, but in the Agamas, the specialists are referred to as "Gurukal" or "Diksha". According to the Agamas, Gurukal or Diksha are open to all men and women and there is no restriction. The male assistants in the temples are called *pandarams* and female assistants who prepare the lamps, wick, carry them to the shrine, light them and pass them to the Gurukal are referred to as "the slaves of Rudra".

The core of Hinduism is in the Agamas and the core of the Agamas is in the temples and the core of temples is in the deities. All the rituals in temples we see today are dictated by the Agamas.

1.3 The Ramayana and the Mahabharata

Following the Upanishads comes the epics — the *Ramayana* and the *Mahabharata*. These two epics are a source of inspiration and direction to the Hindu way of life. Within each epic there are shorter stories, tales and discourses on subjects that pertain to the present-day life situations.

The *Ramayana* is not a mere story of Rama and Sita that took place during 7400 BC, but it is a story that we live every moment of our lives. The epic narrates the story of Rama, the prince of Kosala; his banishment from the kingdom by his father, King Dasharatha; his travel across India with his wife Sita and brother Lakshmana; the kidnapping of his wife by the demon king of Sri Lanka, Ravana, resulting in war and finally, the killing of Ravana and returning to Ayodhya with Sita to be crowned king. For Hindus, Lord Ram is an *Avatar*. Avatar translates as "descent" and refers to the appearance or reincarnation of God on earth, for the sake of his devotees, to restore order and moral.

In the *Ramayana,* there are shorter stories and tales, which are universal and guide us as to how we should behave and conduct our lives under various circumstances. The *Ramayana* is still very relevant to the present-day society, as the epic has important lessons to offer in all facets of the civilization including in areas as diverse as the art of government administration. For example, it details the advanced political organisation that existed in Ayodhya to provide maximum happiness to maximum people for a maximum period based on the principle of Dharma. King Rama signalled man's ability to govern nations.

On the other hand, the *Mahabharata* literally means a great story. It is a story of the dynamic wars that took place around 5000 years ago, between two related families, the Pandavas and the Kauravas, over a kingdom in northern India. Within the *Mahabharata* is the dialogue between Lord Krishna and the warrior prince Arjuna. In this dialogue, Krishna expounds lucidly the fundamentals of Hindu religion and Hindu Dharma. For Hindus, Lord Krishna is an avatar, an incarnation of God. This dialogue is referred to as the *Bhagavad Gita.*

1.4 The Bhagavad Gita

The *Bhagavad Gita* is a unique book for all ages. Its teachings are universal and belong to all human beings and not to any religion, cult or country.

Very few Hindus would have read the Vedas, the Upanishads or the Agamas, but almost all Hindus know the basic storyline of the *Ramayana* and the *Mahabharata*. The *Bhagavad Gita* is a chapter within the *Mahabharata*, a dialogue between Lord Krishna and the Pandava prince Arjuna at Kurukshetra, amidst the great war between the Pandavas and the Kauravas. During this dialogue, Lord Krishna reveals the spiritual truth of Yoga, Vedanta, Bhakti and Karma to a confused and reluctant Arjuna. All these teachings of Lord Krishna were later recorded by Sage Vyasa as the Divine Songs or the Bhagavad (given by the Lord) Gita (songs), consisting of eighteen chapters with 700 Sanskrit verses.

For present-day Hindus, the *Bhagavad Gita* represents a book that could be considered as an equivalent to other religious texts, like the Bible.

1.5 The Puranas

The Puranas are scriptures composed after the epics, the *Mahabharata* and the *Ramayana*. They elaborate on the hymns, philosophies and rituals mentioned in the Vedas. The Puranas contain every type of knowledge from cosmology to gardening. Some of the Puranas deal in detail with the characters in the epics. For example, the *Bhagavata Purana* describes the life of lord Krishna.

1.6 Summary

Although the above scriptures and epics provide the basis for the practice, unlike most religions, there is no specific structure for worship in Hinduism. No individual or prophet has founded it. There is also no authority figure or a core set of texts to follow. The other major religions are dated in a way that you can go back to the origin. But, Hinduism emerges from the mist of time and it is a synthesis of a variety of religious experiences and offers a complete view of life.

The practice of Hinduism keeps evolving with the times. The rituals, customs and beliefs have survived not only in the temples, but also in millions of households. Hinduism allows freedom of thought and is not bound by a particular set of beliefs or rituals.

Hinduism is god-centered, unlike most other religions, which are generally prophet-centred. Hinduism is based on internal principals that apply to all human beings.

"The three essentials of Hinduism are belief in God, in the Vedas as revelation, in the doctrine of karma and transmigration."

— Swami Vivekananda

2

THE CONCEPT OF GOD IN HINDUISM

There is a misconception that Hindus pray to several gods. But in fact, Hindus believe in a Supreme God whose qualities and form are represented by a multitude of deities. Hinduism is a monotheist religion. There is only one god and that god resides within everyone and in everything, from inert material to living beings. He is universal.

According to Hinduism, the entire universe is God in the form of the Supreme Being. He envelops the whole cosmos and transcends to infinity.

In the Upanishads it is said: "God who is both within and without pervades the whole universe. He is moving and unmoving. He is far and near, and within all these and without all these."

Therefore, the Hindus consider everything as manifestations of God — including plants, trees, the sun and moon, animals and humans.

The Hindus respect all religions and believe that the realisation of divinity is the aim of all religions. Like rivers with different names finally flowing into the ocean and emerging as one, religions may take different paths but finally lead to the same ocean of divinity — God. Krishna makes this clear in the *Bhagavad Gita*, chapter 7, verse 21 & 22, as follows:

"Whosoever desires to worship whatever deity using any name, form and method with faith, I make the faith steady in that very deity. Endowed with steady faith they worship that deity and obtain their wishes through that deity. Those wishes are indeed granted by Me."

In Hinduism, God is universal, absolute and eternal from which all things emanate and to which all return. All human beings are divine and all are essentially one. Everything is connected and the same God resides in every human being as atman or *atma*, the eternal self.

The Indian sage, Ramana Maharshi, mentioned that of all the definitions of GOD, "none is indeed so well put as the biblical statement: *I AM THAT I AM."*

In the *Bhagavad Gita*, chapter 10, verse 20, Krishna amplifies this concept to Arjuna as follows:

"I am the ultimate consciousness situated within the heart of all living entities and I am the beginning, the middle and the end as well of all living entities."

According to Swami Chinmayananda, "Love is the very basis of Hinduism. If you know how to love, then you are a Hindu. All great people became great because of their love for others. They gained greatness because they learnt to love."

The basic texts in Hinduism provide different spiritual concepts and paths to achieve liberation but do not impose any specific path on the follower. As a result, the faith allows freedom of thought. No Hindu is bound to accept any particular set of beliefs or rituals. It is left to the individual to reflect upon and think, investigate and inquire about the spiritual ideas and concepts provided by the scriptures, and select and accept what suits him best. Therein lies the glory and greatness of Hinduism. It allows diverse views and tolerates diversity, not only internally but also externally.

Chapter 3

THE CONCEPT
OF HINDU MURTIS

Hinduism has an ancient and extensive tradition rooted in iconography. In Hinduism, an image of God represents emotional and religious values. A *murti* (idol) in itself is not the god it represents, but a symbol that reminds of something emotional and of real value to the worshiper.

Symbolism is a part of human vocabulary that expresses and reveals what common words cannot. Symbols add new dimensions and significance to the reality and meaning of things. When words fail to express one's thoughts, then symbols come to the rescue. For example, a chemical formula representing a substance cannot be described fully in words but it has a special significance and understanding to the scientist. Similarly symbols play an important part in Hinduism, which recognises that all finite things are symbols of infinite. For a Hindu worshiper, a *murti* represents certain aspects of God and helps him to see abstract phenomena in concrete objects.

A *murti* of a Hindu deity is typically made from clay, by welding metals, or by carving stone or wood.

The Hindu concept of God is based on the idea of a trinity — Brahma, Vishnu and Siva (Mahesh), who is responsible for the creation, preservation and destruction, in that order. This correlates to Christianity's concept of its holy trinity: the Father, the Son and the Holy Spirit.

In Hinduism, there's no order in the worship of idols. One can say it is similar to a ministerial set up with a Supreme Deity surrounded by sub deities allocated with particular aspects of divinity. In this ministerial order, goddesses like Lakshmi, Durga, Saraswati, etc., would be considered as sub deities with particular divinities attributed to them. For example, Lakshmi is the goddess of wealth, Durga is the warrior goddess and Saraswati is the goddess of knowledge.

Similarly, the followers of Shaivism or the Shaiva tradition consider Lord Siva as their Supreme God and Ganesh and Murugan as their sub deities. In the same way, followers of Lord Krishna or the Vaishnavites consider Krishna as the Supreme God and have similar sub deities. However, the Hindus are free to pray to any of the deities in temples dedicated to any of one of these gods whenever they wish to do so.

In Ceylon (Sri Lanka) during the British rule, Protestant missionaries attacked the practice of idol worship and temple rituals as devilish and of no value. Arumugam Palli (1822-1879) from Jaffna, Ceylon, more commonly recognised as **Arumuga Navalar**, demonstrated to the Christians that Christianity and Jesus himself were rooted in the temple rituals of the ancient Israelites. He had received the title '*Navalar*' or 'learned' from the Siva monastery in Tanjavore, India, for his work in religious revivalism. Arumugam Navalar was able to prove this successfully because he studied at the Protestant Christian Jaffna Central School and became an English and Tamil teacher at the same school where Reverend Peter Percival was the principal. He had assisted Reverend Peter Percival in translating the Kings James Bible into Tamil.

Navalar left teaching and conducted weekly sermons at Hindu temples throughout Jaffna and South India explaining the concept of worship in Hindu temples with reference to the Agamas. He also travelled to India and established Hindu schools and published Hindu religious books. He set up a printing press in Jaffna to print palm-leaf originals of ancient Tamil literature and Hindu religious books so that they can be used in schools. The Hindu school he established at Chidambaram in Tamil Nadu, India, in 1965 is still functioning. If not for Navalar's intervention, the conversion of the Hindus to Protestant Christianity in Jaffna would have continued unabated.

The following are some of the examples of Hindu *murtis* and what they represent.

Brahma

3.1 Brahma is believed to be the creator of the universe and a member of the Hindu trinity. He is attributed with having four heads and they represent the four Vedas and the four yugas. Brahma mode of transport is a swan. He carries a book in one hand symbolising the Vedas.

However, Lord Brahma should not be confused with Brahman, which refers to the Supreme Being, God.

The concept of Brahma is found mainly in the scriptures. There are only a few temples dedicated to Brahma and he is generally not worshiped in temples and homes as extensively as the other *murtis*, such as Siva, Krishna or Ganesh.

A 2000-year-old temple dedicated to Brahma is in Pushkar, Rajasthan, and it was rebuilt in 14 AD after it was destroyed by the Muslim invaders. The only other known temples dedicated to Brahma are in Tamil Nadu and Uttar Pradesh in India. There is one in Central Java, Indonesia, but it is dedicated to Brahma as well as Vishnu and Siva.

Vishnu

3.2 Vishnu is the second member of the Hindu holy trinity. He has taken several incarnations, the most famous ones being that of Rama and Krishna. He is also known as Narayana and Hari and is conceived as the Preserver or the Protector. In Hindu religious texts, he is described as having dark blue complexion symbolising his cosmic dimensions and connection with rain, thunder and the earth. Garuda, the king of birds, is his vehicle.

His four hands hold *sankha* (conch), chakra (discus), *gada* (mace) and *padma* (lotus).

Conch symbolises the sacred sound 'OM';

Discus symbolises the cyclic nature of existence, the destruction of evil and the protection of the rightness;

Mace symbolises the power of knowledge and

Lotus symbolises beauty, harmony and self-realisation.

Siva

3.3 Mahesh (Siva) is the third god in the Hindu trinity. Mahesh is another name for Siva (Shiva). 'Siva' means "the auspicious one".

He represents both the death that destroys, and the reproduction that follows destruction. Siva is symbolised by a *lingam*, the emblem of supreme.

Siva is said to have three eyes and with the third eye he can see the past, present and the future. His weapon is a three-pronged trident that represents his ability to create, destroy and regenerate. His mode of transport is the bull, Nandi.

Saraswati

3.4 Saraswati is considered as the consort of Brahma and is revered as the goddess of knowledge, arts and speech. She is the patron of all intellectual endeavours. Those who pursue learning hold her in high reverence and seek her blessings. Her picture can be seen in schools and universities that follow the Hindu tradition.

She wears a white saree and is seated on a white lotus flower symbolising light, knowledge and truth.

Like her consort, Brahma, she also uses the swan as her vehicle.

She is always seen playing the musical instrument, veena, which represents the creative arts and science.

The book she holds in one hand stands for the Vedas, the divine knowledge; and the crystal mala in the other hand symbolise the power of meditation.

Lakshmi

3.5 Lakshmi is the consort of Vishnu and is revered as the goddess of beauty, good fortune and prosperity.

She sits on a red lotus flower and uses the owl as her vehicle.

She is also referred to as Sri (Shri), which refers to all qualities that is feminine such as grace, beauty, prosperity, etc.

The Hindu festival of Diwali, the festival of lights, is celebrated in November every year. On the third day of Diwali, the night of *Amavasya*, holds great significance in the worship of Goddess Lakshmi, for it is believed to be the joyous day when Sri showers bestows her blessings of prosperity on mankind. Her four hands represent the four goals in life namely, Dharma (moral), Kama (love), Artha (wealth) and Moksha (liberation). The same way, the red lotus flower she sits on and the red saree she wears stands for beauty and wealth.

Parvati

3.6 Parvati

Parvati is the consort of Lord Siva and is literally worshipped as the other half of Siva. She is considered as the family goddess by many Hindus. She is also called Shakti, which means power — the cosmic energy that represent the dynamic force that moves the entire universe. She can change form and be both benevolent and destructive, like her spouse. She is also known as Durga a name she acquired after killing the demon Durg. She is also worshipped as Kali in her destructive form.

As the goddess of family and love, people pray to her for her help in matters related to marriage, parenting and fertility. Women worship goddess Pravati for getting good partners and a happy married life.

A lion is her mode of transport.

During the Navaratri (nine nights) festival in the month of November, people fast and offer prayers to her for her blessing.

She symbolises noble virtues and her red saree represents purity and power.

Ganesh

3.7 Lord Ganesh

The elephant-headed god is the son of Siva and Parvati. He is portrayed with a pot belly, a broken tusk, with four hands holding a *pasam*, a goad and a pot of sweet rice in each and the fourth one bestowing blessings. Ganesh is one of the most-worshiped deities in Hinduism. He is the remover of all obstacles and is therefore worshiped first when visiting temples and before starting any ventures.

A *pasam* in his hand is a triple-twine weapon, which represents arrogance, illusion (maya) and ignorance.

The goad is to remind how one should steer the soul away from all the ignorance and illusions.

His elephant head stands for unusually high intelligence and his large ears represent the power of keen hearing and the tusk for the ability to discriminate.

There's an interesting story behind his broken tusk. According to the tale, Ganesha was assisting Sage Vyasa in writing down the story of Mahabharata, as the sage narrated it. So when the pen he was writing with broke, Ganesha snapped his own tusk and used it as a pen so that the writing of the story could continue without any interruption. The broken tusk symbolises sacrifice and also establishes Ganesh as the patron of the arts and letters.

Murugan

3.8 Lord Murugan (Skanda)

Murugan was created from six sparks emanated from Lord Siva's third eye. These sparks were carried by the god of fire (Agni) to the river Ganges who then carried them to the pond Saranavan. In this pond, from the six sparks, arose six babies. Six maidens known as Karthigai Pengal found the babies in the pond and brought them up and when all six were later handed to Parvati (Siva's consort), they fused together to form one baby. He is therefore known as Shunmugha or 'the one with six faces'.

Shanmugha's six heads symbolise the five senses and the mind that controls them.

The three important and integral aspects of Murugan's appearance are his spear (*vel*) in his hand, his peacock mount and the rooster adorning his banner.

His *vel* signifies the power of wisdom. His mother Parvati gifted him this spear when he defeated the asuras in a battle.

Peacock symbolizes his destruction of the ego and the rooster proclaims loudly the parnava mantra, Om.

Murugan is considered as the patron god of Tamilians and so temples dedicated to him are popular in areas where there's significant Tamil population, say, in Tamil Nadu, Sri Lanka, Malaysia, Indonesia, Singapore, Canada, United Kingdom and Australia.

For Tamilians, Murugan stands for divine handsomeness, youthfulness, happiness and sweetness.

In Sri Lanka, Murugan is worshiped as Kataragama Deviyo (the lord of Kataragama or Kadigamam) or Kathiravel by both the Singhalese and the Tamils. The prominent Murugan temple in Sri Lanka is in Jaffna, the Nullur Kandasawamy Temple.

In Malaysia, there is the famous Sri Subramanian Batu Cave Temple with a 42.7-metre high Murugan statue placed at the entrance.

Other well-known Murugan shrines around the world are the Sydney Murugan Temple in Australia and the United Kingdom High Gate Murugan Temple.

4

THE WORSHIP OF NAVAGRAHAS (CELESTIAL BODIES)

The Navagrahas (the nine houses) are important deities in Hinduism. The Navagrahas are made of the following:

The Sun and the Moon

The five planets — Mars, Mercury, Jupiter, Venus and Saturn

And the two demon deities — Rahu and Ketu

The two demons' names are derived either from the comets or from the hostile planets of the solar system, Neptune and Pluto. These two deities are considered auspicious or inauspicious depending on their association with the other planets in one's *kundali* or the birth chart.

The Hindus accept that the sun, the moon and the planets influence all life on earth, including the humans. The solar system with its precise orbits and constant motion influences all life-forms. Even a minute variation in the configuration of the planets or the intensity of the energy of the sun will influence earth. Hinduism recognises the energy we receive from the sun and understands that without it there won't be life on earth.

The Navagrahas, therefore, gets an important place, separate from other *murtis* in Hindu temples. At the commencement of any ceremony in the temple, the first offering is to Ganesh, followed by the offerings to the Navagrahas.

Each of the nine Navagrahas is personified as per the influence it exerts. For example, the Sun (Surya), occupies the central position, wearing a golden crown and riding a chariot with seven horses that represent the seven colours of the sunlight.

The Moon is called Chandra in Sanskrit and represents the mind (mental stability), beauty and happiness.

Navagrahas

Mars is called Mangala and rules the muscular and circulatory systems in the human body.

Mercury is called Buddha and represents intelligence and communication, and rules the nervous system.

Jupiter is known as Brihaspati and symbolises knowledge, love and spirituality. It rules the kidney, liver and the arterial system.

Venus is called Shukra and symbolises love and passion.

Saturn is called Shani and is regarded as a troublesome deity whose influence in the planetary system can interfere with one's fortune. Shani stands for longevity, misery and grief. If one is under the influence of Shani, the Hindus believe fasting on Saturdays and offering donations to the poor, along with prayers, will help negate its ill effects.

Rahu and Ketu are the shadow planets as mentioned earlier and they could have good and adverse effects on one's path to success.

5

THE SIGNIFICANCE OF OM

In Hinduism, 'Om' reflects the primordial sound associated with the creation of the universe from nothing, because in the beginning there was no hard matter and only darkness. The combination of very minute atom resulted in the generation of heat and the formation of hard matter. This caused an explosion, the Big Bang, and the matter spread all over the universe. The Hindus believe that the sound that emanated during the Big Bang is the Pranava Mantra or Omkara, the primordial sound.

The syllable 'Om' is described in various ways in the Vedas and in the early Upanishads. These descriptions include the atman (the soul), the infinite, the truth, and the ultimate reality.

Om (Aum) is the most sacred word and the most important symbol in Hinduism.

It is a part of the iconography found in the ancient and medieval era, in the manuscripts, temples and monasteries of Buddhism, Jainism and Sikhism. Om has a spiritual meaning in all Indian Dharma. Epigraphical variations of Om are found in many Asian countries.

Following are the examples of various scripts in which Om is written:

Sanskrit

Tamil

Chinese

Indonesian

Japanese

The symbol of Om is also found on coins. For example, coins that dates back to 1st and 4th century CE embossed with Om along with other symbols are found in Sri Lanka.

In the *Bhagavad Gita,* in chapter 8, verse 13 and in chapter 17, verse 24, Krishna speaks about Om. Translations of the verses are as follows:

> *Anyone uttering the indestructible monosyllable Om, transcendental sound vibration of the*

Ultimate Truth, remembering Me continuously; thus relinquishing their body in this way achieves the supreme goal.

Therefore, in accordance to the ordinances of the Vedic scriptures, duties based on sacrifice, charity and austerity, by followers of Vedanta and the Ultimate Truth always begin well by pronouncing OM the eternal, transcendental sound vibration of the Ultimate Consciousness.

Om is the predominant force of power and for this reason, as per the Vedic scriptures, the chanting of Om, a minimum of three times, before every auspicious activity is essential. It must be chanted with a high and prolonged note, and with great devotion. Chanting of this mantra creates a sensation in every part of the body. One forgets worldly thoughts and invokes their dominant inner strength. Chanting Om several times, say 3, 9, 11, 21 or even 108 times a day, will remove sadness and disappointments and make one content.

Even scientists (Ajay Anil Gurjor et al 2009, B N Gangaahar et al 2011 and Gabriel Axel 2013) agree that chanting 'Om' cleanses the brain and promotes wellbeing.

The sound produced is very important when chanting 'Om' because it can bring about a transformation within the chanter, leading to the awakening of inner power and strength. The syllable Om has three sounds:

The "ahh" sound should come from deep within the abdomen.

The "ooh" sound should produce the feeling of vibration in the chest and neck.

With the final "mmm" sound, one should feel the vibration in the head and neck with the lips closed.

There is a fourth sound associated with the chanting of Om — the silence after the sound "mmm". At this moment of silence, there is a vibration in each person participating in the chanting, highlighting the pure consciousness of the self:

Sat Chit Anandam — I exist; I know I am bliss.

6

THE CONCEPT OF CREATION

Evolution in Hinduism is an integral and natural aspect of creation. Hinduism explains the process of evolution from a wider perspective. It goes beyond what is visible to the naked eye to explain the mechanism responsible for creating not only the world but also the whole universe.

The Hindus conceive creation as an ongoing cycle of formation and destruction. Hinduism is dedicated to the idea that the cosmos itself undergoes an immense number of deaths and rebirths. The length of the evolutionary journey boggles the mind. Sri Sathya Sai Baba, the famous godman, explains that the journey starts when life is formed as granite and then evolves from granite to vegetation, to animal, to human, to super human, to cosmic, and then to the divine.

According to the Hindu scriptures, the life cycle of the world is divided into four yugas (eras):

Sathya Yuga (The Golden Age),

Treta Yuga (The Silver Age),

Dwapara Yuga (The Copper Age), and

Kali Yuga (The Iron Age or the Era of Machinery).

We are in the last era, the Kali Yuga, which started in year 3102 BC, at the end of Mahabharata, and it will last for 432,000 human years. The Hindus believe that at the end of this era, the world will come to an end and there will be another new beginning.

Most Hindus believed in the theory of biological evolution long before Charles Darwin's Theory of Evolution. According to the Hindu scriptures, one has to take several births, 8,400,000 births in total, before taking on the form of a human being. Life is a progression from the microscopic life-form to the higher order of animals. The scriptures state that there are 3,000,000 births in plant life, 2,700,000 births in insect life, 1,400,000 as birds, 900,000 as fish and 400,000 as animals. Therefore, it is a great fortune to attain the human form through this biological evolution.

Human form is the pinnacle of the evolution. Through this form, one can attain knowledge, devotion and detachment. The human body is also considered as a temple as it houses the atman. However, the *Bhagavad Gita* states that one should not develop attachment to the body, or consider it as the true self. People who identify with the body as real remain ignorant of their spiritual nature and suffer fear and anxiety about their wellbeing and morality. A karma yogi who keeps his body and mind under control and engages his body in action without desire, offering the fruits of his action to God, living only to perform his bodily functions, becomes liberated from the bondage of birth and death.

In the *Bhagavad Gita*, chapter 2, verse 47, states:

> *Thy right is to work only, but never with its fruits;*
> *let not the fruits of action be thy motive, nor let thy*
> *attachment be in action.*

In chapter 8, verse 5, Krishna also states that, "The one who remembers me at the moment of death, relinquishes the body and ascends and achieves *my nature.*"

7

REVERENCES TO NATURE

Hindus have always had great respect for Mother Nature, including the sun, the moon, other plants and all life-forms on earth. In the puranas and other scriptures, great importance has been attributed to plants as they form the foundation of life. Even, special status is granted to some plants. A few familiar plants with distinct reverence are:

Banyan tree (Ficus *india*),

***Bo* tree or peepal tree** (Ficus *religiosa*),

***Audumbar* tree** (Ficus *racemosa*),

Banana plant (Musa *acuminate*),

Mango tree ((Mangifera *indica*)

Coconut tree (Cocos *nucifira*), and

Tulsi plant (Ocimum *tenuiflorum*).

The peepal and *audumbar* trees are 24-hour oxygen generators and are very important for the ecological balance. The Hindus revere these trees and in order to protect these trees, they are associated with some of the Hindu deities.

The Bo tree (Bodhi or peepal , Ficus *religiosa*) has as special place in Buddhism because it is believed that under the peepal or bo tree Prince Siddhartha meditated, attained enlightenment and became a Buddha. This peepal tree under which Buddha meditated is in Bodh Gaya, Bihar, India. In 288 BC, Sanghamittra, the daughter of King Asoka, brought a branch of this tree to Sri Lanka and planted it in Anuradhapura.

It's been growing continually till this day. The bark and the leaves of this peepal are considered auspicious and used in various religious ceremonies.

Likewise, banana leaves are considered clean and pure, and food and offerings are served on it.

Leaves of the Bo tree

The bark, wood and leaves of the mango tree are used in a variety of Hindu prayers and ceremonies.

The purna kumbha (*kumbam* in Tamil) signifies the idea that human beings are a part of nature. This is an essential segment of the Hindu worship. *Purna kumbha* literally means "a full vessel" and it is a symbol of abundance, wisdom, immortality and the "source of life" as mentioned in the Vedas.

The purna kumbha starts with a pot filled with water. The mouth of the pot is covered with a husked coconut and the sides are decorated with mango leaves. This pot is then placed on top of a banana leaf or on a tray.

The mango leaf is associated with Kama, the god of love, the coconut represents prosperity and

Water represents the life-giving ability of nature.

Rice, flowers and fruits are also placed around the pot. The items used as a part of the *purna kumbha* symbolise the human being's relationship with nature, and when nature thrives, human beings too flourish.

The *purna kumbha* is used in Hindu temples and in Hindu religious ceremonies. It can also be placed at the entrance of the house as a welcome gesture.

Purna Kumbha

TULSI PLANT

Tulsi (Ocimum *tenuiflorum*) or holy basil is a sacred plant in Hindu belief and is considered as the holiest of all plant species. The Puranas say that where there is a garden of tulsi plants, that place is considered sacred and the air that carries the fragrance of tulsi benefits people who come into contact with it.

This plant is associated with Lord Krishna and is offered to him during prayers and temple ceremonies.

Medicinally, the tulsi extract is excellent for mental and physical health and wellbeing. Tulsi improves the immune system, and promotes vigor and vitality. It is considered to have antibacterial properties and is good for respiratory tract problems such as coughs and colds. It purifies the air.

Tulse Tree

It is extensively used in Ayurveda. The plant is effective even if it is not consumed, because even being in its proximity is enough to promote good health. If one wants to consume tulsi leaves, it should not be chewed, as the mercury in it will affect the teeth enamel. It should only be swallowed with fresh water.

According to the Hindu belief, it is important to have at least one tulsi plant in the courtyard of the house.

The Hindus also revere all living forms, be it animals, birds, fishes and insects. Reverence to all life-forms by Hindus comes from the teaching that all life was created for the purpose of emotional and physical support of the human beings.

The Hindus consider cow as the most sacred animal because it provides milk, from which a variety of foods are produced. Milk and ghee are also used in religious ceremonies. The bull, the male of the species, has helped farmers to till the land for thousand of years.

Animals and insects help mankind in a variety of ways. For example, sheep provides wool, silkworm provides silk, bee provides honey and so on. Living in harmony with all life-forms is an essential part of the Hindu existence. In return, the animals also show their love and devotion toward humans, promoting harmony in the world.

8

PREFERENCE TO
A VEGETARIAN DIET

Diet in Hinduism is as varied as its diverse traditions. All ancient Hindu religious texts strongly recommend a vegetarian diet based on the principle of non-violence (ahimsa) against all life-forms.

The Hindu scriptures also state that all of creation is a vast food chain; the cosmos is a giant food cycle.

However, the main reason for a vegetarian diet among the Hindus is the principle of non-violence towards animals. In keeping with the principle of ahimsa, the food offered to the deities is also vegetarian. It is the practice of the Hindus to offer food to the deities and receive it back as prasad (*prasadam* in Tamil) or sanctified food.

The followers of Hinduism also consider a non-vegetarian diet detrimental to their spiritual development. As a consequence, many Hindus prefer a lacto-vegetarian diet, which include milk-based food and other non-animal derived food, excluding meat and egg. This form of vegetarian diet also assists in the harmony of food production with nature, whilst being respectful to other life-forms on earth.

In addition to being vegetarian, Hindus also fast on particular days of the week (days that are attributed to their favourite deities), or during a particular religious festival such as the Navratri, the nine nights in November, when Goddess Durga is worshipped with vigour. The important aspect of the fast is the devotion to a particular cause. The purpose of the fasting is also symbolic self-control and self-purification. Fasting also helps to remove toxins from the body, thereby aiding the mind and body in feeling better.

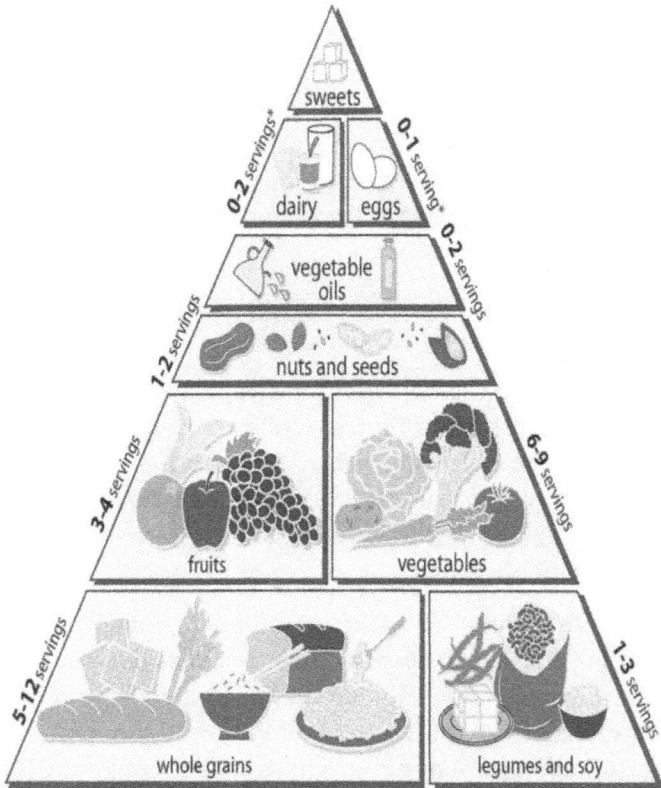

Loma Linda University Vegetarian Food Pyramid

According to the *Rig Veda*,

> *Mankind develops the ability for progressive living*
> *through fasts that serve as initiation (diksha).*

The Loma Linda University's Vegetarian Food Pyramid, presented at the Third International Conference on Vegetarian Nutrition, is shown above (Haddad Ella H et al). Hindus consider egg (shown in the pyramid) as non-vegetarian.

With the influence of the western civilization, many Hindus are now non-vegetarian. Most non-vegetarian Hindus generally avoid beef, as cow is considered very sacred in Hinduism. Some non-vegetarian Hindus also revert to vegetarian diet during certain days of the week — on the days that are devoted to their deities and during religious festivals.

Scientists such as Milton R Mills, MD and Shivam Joshi MD are now finding evidence that human anatomy is better adopted for processing plant food rather than meat. Human intestinal tracts are much longer, similar to that of herbivorous animals. This gives more time to break down the plant food and absorb its nutrients. As opposed to this, carnivores have a short intestinal tract and strong stomach acid that breaks down meat and kills harmful bacteria.

In humans, the stomach acid is weak and therefore there is a need to cook the meat before eating. When too much animal protein is consumed, the body has trouble in eliminating all the waste. Dr. Milton R. Mills provides some evidence of this in his article 'The Comparative Anatomy of Eating', published in 2012.

9
PRAYERS

Praying to God is a part of the Hindu way of life. For Hindus, prayer is a way of expressing their faith and devotion to God. It is a routine for most followers of the faith.

The practice of worshipping deities at home remains at the heart of Hinduism. Almost every Hindu home has a small shrine with a sacred space reserved for prayers, where small images or idols of the deities are placed Hindus are free to choose their favorite deity (*murti*) to pray to. Many believers pray to several deities at the same time. However, essentially all prayers start off with the prayer to Ganesh, the remover of obstacles.

A Small Shrine with Deties

Besides the deities, it is customary to have a plate (*thali*) in front of the *murtis* to offer flowers, fruits and other offerings while praying. A source of light, like an oil lamp or candle or an electric light is also usually present in these pooja rooms. Some people also keep a small bell, small bowls containing holy ash, sandalwood paste or *tilak*, and incense. The offering of flowers is akin to saying that our life should be like flowers; life should blossom and be colourful, spread fragrance everywhere and be of service to others.

The pooja or prayer secession commences with the lighting of a lamp.

The oil used in the lamp represents human tendencies.

The wick symbolises the ego.

The flame, which always goes upwards, represents knowledge. Knowledge drains the oil (innate tendencies) as it burns and destroys the wick (ego).

The light from the lamp stands for knowledge, which removes ignorance like how the light removes darkness. Anything can be achieved in life by acquiring knowledge.

For conducting poojas, a lamp with ghee is preferred as it attracts more *sattvik* (good qualities) vibrations than an ordinary oil lamp. When ghee lamp is burning, the flame attacks *raja* particles in the atmosphere and the enhanced vibration of these particles spreads over a larger area. These vibrations last for a longer period than a particle attacked by the ordinary lamp, even after the flame is extinguished.

Ghee Wick Lamps

After lighting the lamp, a bell is rung to invite the deity and accept the prayers. The sound of the bell not only invites the deities but also drives away evil spirits and keeps out irrelevant noises and comments from other worshipers.

A well-designed bell made from an alloy of different metals, including cadmium, copper, zinc and nickel will produce the long vibration of the sound 'Om'.

After lighting the lamp and ringing the bell, the prayer commences with the chanting of 'Om' a minimum of three times, followed by a prayer to Lord Ganesh.

Finally, the prayer is concluded with an *aarti*. This involves circulating a lighted lamp around the deity in a clockwise direction, normally seven times or more, accompanied by singing the praises of the same deity.

The Camphor Lamp

Aarti is an expression of many things — it could signify the removal of darkness at the end of a prayer or bhajan session, or the feeling of love and gratitude towards God, depending on the situation. The *aarti* also represents our daily activities, which revolves around God and signifies that one is peripheral to divinity and reminds us to keep our ego in check and be humble, regardless of our social status. During a prayer ceremony, the person performing the *aarti* finally circulates the flame to all that are present. The devotees cup their hands over the flame and raise them to their foreheads. This gesture signifies that the blessing has passed from the deity to the flame and then to the devotees.

The *aarti* ceremony dates back to the ancient concept of fire rituals. In Sanskrit, "Aa" means complete and "rti" means love, so *aarti* is 'complete love to God'. A traditional *aarti* ritual is performed with several items —flowers to represent the earth, water and cloth to represent the water element, a fan or a yak-tail fan to signify the space and the precious quality of air, incense representing purified mind and intelligence, and the flame representing the fire element. The *aarti* is usually performed using lighted camphor or a ghee lamp with one, three or five wicks.

After completing the *aarti,* one applies *vibhuti*, sandalwood paste and/or *tilak* on the forehead (between the eyebrows) of the devotee. The space between the eyebrows is considered to be the location of the third eye. It is also the location of a major nerve centre. Applying *tilak* at this spot retains vitality and prevents negative energy from entering the body.

Aarti is not only limited to divinity but can be performed on all forms of life, even on inanimate objects like machines. It is performed on individuals as a mark of respect or as a welcome gesture. The *aarti* is carried out on machines as a prayer so that the object helps one to excel in its designated activity.

Vibhuti is obtained from the residue of the sacrificial fire where sandalwood, along with ghee and other herbs, are offered in worship, or it is obtained by the burning of cow dung and/ or rice husk.

Sathya Sai Baba, the Indian guru, used to produce *vibhuti* from thin air with the wave of his hand and used to give this to his devotees to eat. *Vibhuti*, when consumed, imparts the blessing of the divine.

The direction in which we apply the *vibhuti* on the forehead (which is considered a religious symbol) also reveals the particular deity one worships. Worshipers of Lord Siva apply three horizontal lines of *vibhuti* on the forehead, and devotes of Vishnu apply two vertical lines, U-shaped, on the forehead.

When one applies *vibhuti* on the forehead with three lines and a red *tilak*, as shown, it symbolises Siva–Shakti, the union of energy and the matter that creates the entire universe.

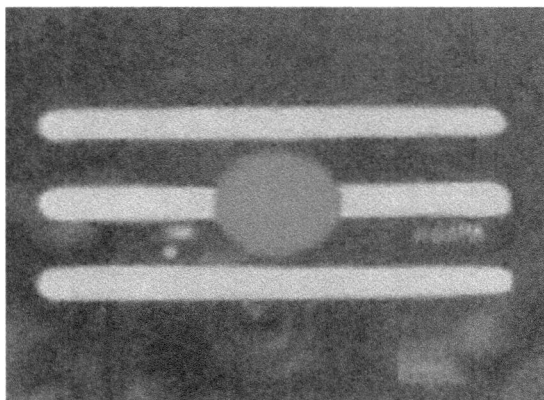

In Sanskrit, *vibhuti* means eternal, supreme, etc., and it stands for power and the divine. Applying *vibhuti* denotes the destruction of illusion by reminding us of the transient nature of all things. It also reminds us of the temporary nature of our lives — that all life eventually ends in ashes.

Likewise, sandalwood represents our lives, which should spread fragrance and happiness.

The turmeric–lime mixture for *tilak* has medicinal properties. It is good for the skin and helps to develop harmony within the nerves. Turmeric is also a good blood purifier.

10

THE AMAZING
POWER OF PRAYERS

Prayer is a way of communicating one's thoughts with the Infinite Intelligence or God, which responds to the nature of your thoughts and beliefs. There is nothing that cannot be achieved with prayer. Remember that with God, all things are possible.

People of all religions have believed and still believe in the miraculous power of prayer. In the Gospel of Mathew (Mathew 21:22) it says:

> *"And all things, whatsoever ye shall ask in prayer, believing, ye shall receive."*

In the *Bhagavad Gita*, chapter 9, verses 29 & 30, Krishna highlights the importance of prayer as follows:

> *"Even if a wicked sinner worships Me with pure devotion, he should be considered a saint because he has correctly resolved that there is nothing better than devoted worship of God."*

In chapter 18, verse 46, Krishna again states:

> *"Through one's good deeds and prayers to God, an individual finds divine contentment and salvation."*

It is important to remember that with prayer one can achieve anything.

Mahatma Gandhi's view on prayer was as follows:

> *"Prayer has been the saving of my life. Without it I would have been a lunatic long ago. My*

autobiography will tell you that I have had my fair share of the bitterest public and private experiences. They threw me into temporary despair, but if I was able to get rid of it, it was because of prayer."

"God answers prayer in His own way, not ours. His ways are different from the ways of mortals. Hence, they are inscrutable. Prayer presupposes faith. No prayer goes in vain. Prayer is like any other action. It bears fruit whether we see it or not, and the fruit of heart prayer is far more potent than action so-called."

Praying in groups and singing of devotional songs together is a powerful and inspiring experience for Hindus. Group prayers bring people with similar devotion to God together. Group prayers create powerful vibrations because several minds come together for a common cause and therefore are more effective than individual worship.

Bhajans are a form of group prayer. For example, at a Sai Centre bhajan session, the lead singer introduces each line of the devotional song (bhajan), which is then repeated in chorus by the rest of the group. At the end of the song, the lead singer repeats the lines, from the start, to an increased tempo for all to sing again. Finally, the first line of the song is sung slowly by the worshippers. A group prayer session starts with the recital of 'Om' several times — 3 or 9 usually, followed by a devotional song praising Lord Ganesh and then other songs worshipping other deities, sung by different devotees. The group prayer ends with the recitation of mantras, *aarti* and the serving of holy ash and *Prasad*. It is also customary for Hindus to clap their hand while singing devotional songs in a group. As birds fly away from the branches of trees hearing the claps, one's ignorance too vanishes with the clapping of hands in rhythm. It is also believed that clapping of the hands physically stimulates the nerves in the palms, which in turn rouses the internal organs, improving the blood circulation and breathing. Quick movement of the hands stimulates the whole body, helping the heart, lungs and kidney to function better.

In addition to singing devotional songs, Hindus also chant mantras and meditate, as a form of prayer.

A prayer can be very simple, short or long, and is a way of expressing gratitude for everything God has blessed us with.

A Simple Prayer Could Be:

Example 1

O God,
Lead me from the unreal to real,
Lead me from darkness to light,
Lead me from morality to immorality,
Om – peace, peace, peace.

Example 2 (Prayer provided by Sathya Sai Baba)

O Lord, take my love and let it flow in fullness of devotion to Thee.

O Lord, take my hands and let them work incessantly for Thee.

O Lord, take my soul and let it be merged in oneness with Thee.

O Lord, take my mind and thoughts and let them be in tune with Thee.

O Lord, take my everything and let me be an instrument for thy work.

11

MANTRAS

Mantras can be viewed as ancient power words with subtle intentions that keep us connected to the supreme, God, the source of everything.

The word mantra in Sanskrit means the instrument of thought. Mantra could be a word, a verse or a sound (Om) recited or sung several times. For example, each one of the following mantras may be recited several times.

1. **OM, OM, OM...**

2. **OM SAI RAM, OM SAI RAM, OM SAI RAM...**

3. **OM NAMO NARAYANA, OM NAMO NARAYANA, OM NAMO NARAYANA...**

4. **HARI KRISHNA, HARI, KRISHNA, HARI KRISHNA, HARE, HARE.**

5. **HARE RAM, HARE RAM, RAM, RAM, HARE HARE.**

6. **OM NAMOM SIVAYA, OM NAMA SIVAYA, OM NAMA SIVAYA, SIVAYA NAMOM.**

7. **The Gayatri Mantra:**

   > **OM BHUR BHUVAH SUVAH,**
   > **TAT SAVITUR VARENYAM,**
   > **BHARGO DEVASYA DHIMAHI,**
   > **DHIYO YONAH PRACHODAYAT.**

Of all the mantras, the Gayatri Mantra is considered as the most powerful.

Mantras are recited loudly because they release the energy contained in the sound and generate powerful vibrations. These vibrations dispel negative feelings amongst those present and results in the elimination of problems, worries and fears.

12

THE POWER OF MANTRAS

The Hindus chant several mantras that are powerful words.

Spoken words affect us in different ways. Kind words may make us smile, a harsh word could make us angry and as the saying goes:

The word is more powerful than the sword.

Words in the mantras are no different and are selected for their influence and effect. Mantras, when recited or sung as per the prescribed method, have the power to transform people and their lives. They convey a significant meaning and a have a definite effect.

Mantras can be viewed as ancient power words with subtle intentions that keep us connected to God.

Hindus normally receive their mantra from religious gurus, and they then make it a part of their life. Those who do not have a guru may select and chant any of the mantras mentioned in Chapter 10, or those that are popular and time-tested.

It is said that as a first step in establishing a *murti,* the temple priests recite special mantras so that a particular statue can be converted into a living symbol of God. It is only after this act one is allowed to offer prayers to the deity for fruition of his wishes. Such is the power of mantras.

When mantras are recited with devotion, the power of the words creates an extraordinary energy in the inner body and the outer space.

There are a number of mantras recited by the Hindus but none is more powerful than the Gayatri Mantra, as mentioned earlier. The Gayatri Mantra, also known as the Savitri Mantra, is a highly-revered mantra from the *Rigveda*.

In the *Bhagavad Gita* (Chapter 10, verse 30) it says:

"Of the Sama–Veda hymns, I am the Brhat–Sama, also of mantras composed in poetic meter, I am Gayatri."

Buddha praises the Gayatri Mantra as the foremost metre (rhythmic structure).

The Hindu texts state that methodically chanting the Gayatri Mantra removes negative influences, promotes noble thoughts and creativity. It generates self-confidence and contentment amongst others and also protects one from all kind of problems.

The explanation of Gayatri Mantra is as follows:

OM *(God)*

BHUR BHUVAH SUVHA *(Physical and heavenly spheres)*

TAT SAVITUR VARENAYAM *(THAT Adorable Supreme Being from which all are born)*

BHARGO DEVASYA DHIMAHI *(We mediate upon the Spiritual Effulgence of THAT Adorable Supreme Divine Reality)*

DHIYO YONAH PRACHODAYAT *(May that Supreme Divine Being enlighten our intellect.)*

Please note that although the basic translation of the Gayatri Mantra is shown along side each line, there are several condensed versions of the meaning of the Gayatri Mantra.

Swami Vivekananda summarises the meaning of the Gayatri Mantra clearly and simply as follows:

We meditate on the glory of the radiant Being who has produced this universe; may He enlighten our minds.

The Gayatri Mantra is recited a minimum of three times at the end of religious ceremonies, prayers and before beginning mediation. The benefits that one derives from the Gayatri Mantra are found to increase with the number of times it is chanted per day. It is recommended that this mantra be recited in the early morning, at noon and in the evening, for better results.

Hindus have mantras for every important event.

For example:

a)   The mantra, "*Samastah Lokah sukhino bhavantu,*" may be chanted at the end of a prayer secession.

Meaning: May all beings everywhere be happy and free and may thoughts, words, action of my own life contribute in some way to the happiness and to that freedom for all.

b)   The mantra, "*Om gum Ganapataye namah*", is chanted before commencing any major activity, for e.g., work, study, travel, etc., to provide protection and to overcome obstacles.

I bow to the elephant-faced deity, Ganesh, remover of obstacles, with all our existence and accept all his great qualities in our being.

The Mantra SO HUM

I am that I am.

Silently repeating a mantra is a form of meditation. This form of repetition of mantras is also a common practice in Buddhism and Jainism.

Mantra *japa* is a practice of repeating the same mantra silently for an auspicious number of times, say 9, or 108 times, assisted by a *mala* (a chain made of beads). A *mala* used for mantra chanting should consist of 108 beads and a guru (head) bead. When one completes chanting the mantra 108 times by counting the beads in the *mala*, the chain needs to be turned around so that the repetition of the mantra and counting continues without crossing the guru bead. This form of mantra meditation is normally combined with controlled breathing, so that one recites the mantra simultaneously whilst breathing in and out. For example, while chanting the mantra, "SO HUM" one must breathing in at "SO" and breath out at "HAM".

Japa Mala

13
MEDITATION

Sri Sathya Sai Baba has defined meditation as:

"The correct meditation is the merging of all thoughts and feelings in God."

Meditation is a vehicle that carries us across the turbulent seas of our lives to the "other shore" of self-realization.

Our mind experiences continuous flow of thoughts without any order or context, and does not cast away any thoughts but keeps them in the memory. One could say that meditation is a name for a period of rest we give our mind.

Sai Baba

In the *Bhagavad Gita*, chapter 6, verse 10, it says:

> *"One perfecting the science of uniting the individual consciences with the Ultimate Consciousness, consistently residing alone in the secluded place engaged in controlling the mind, desire less free from proprietorship, should mediate on the inner self."*

In chapter 6, verse 16, Krishna also said:

> *"O Arjuna, the science of uniting the individual consciousness with the Ultimate Consciousness never occurs for one who eats too much or one who eats too little, nor also for one who sleeps too much or sleeps too little."*

To practice meditation not only does one needs a healthy body but also a calm mind, sincerity and a burning desire to rise above human imperfections.

The first area of improvement for meditation is that of the body, a cause of many addictions. Good health is maintained by a simple regimen of well-regulated diet, adequate exercise, sleep and relaxation.

Ancient seers practiced meditations in different ways. They could be broadly grouped into three types.

1) Mantra Meditation – Chanting Vedic mantras with concentration

2) Visual Meditation – Meditating on a particular deity.

3) Absorption in mind and heart – Meditation concentrating on one's inner self.

There are also other meditation methods practiced in the context of different cultures, religions and faiths.

In this day and age, one does not have the time or the patience to explore and uncover the ancient meditation techniques before choosing one and adopting it as one's own. Therefore, Sathya Sai Baba has recommended that for today's generation there is only one good and safe meditation method — the ancient meditation technique focusing on light. Baba called this the 'Light Meditation'. Baba has also said that it is safe and effective, and Baba will be our inner guide if we call upon him.

The Light Meditation

The best time for practicing the light meditation is early in the morning but not limited to. Meditation should be avoided after a meal and preferably not within two hours of consuming any type of food. It is a good idea to practice meditation at the same time and at the same place every day.

Before starting meditation, one should take a bath so as to feel clean, fresh, comfortable and relaxed. Then choose a place that is clean and quiet so as to avoid any distractions.

The place chosen for meditation should be slightly elevated from the ground. Place a thick mat on the ground where you can sit comfortably, with your spine erect, in a half lotus position — with your right foot placed over the left foot. If it is physically uncomfortable to sit in a crossed legged position, then you could sit on a chair placed on a mat with your feet resting on the mat. Our ancestors used to sit on a *kusha* grass mats during religious ceremonies and whilst meditating. The mat serves as insulation and thus enhances and maintains the energy generated during meditation.

It is important to hold the back and the neck erect and still, with the right palm placed over the left palm and the thumbs touching each other (the Buddhist method). The eyes must be half or fully closed so that you are not distracted. Then slowly try to relax the whole body starting from the neck, shoulders, hands, chest, teeth, stomach, back and legs.

In the Hindu practice, the hands are placed on the knees with the thumb and forefinger of each hand touching each other, the rest of the fingers extended and the palm open and facing upwards.

Breathe deeply, slowly and evenly for a few minutes, say three minutes, while focusing on the tip of your nose. As you inhale, mentally chant the sound "SO" and as you exhale again mentally chant "HUM". It is not necessary that one should use the mantra "SO-HUM" for this exercise; you could choose any other mantra you are familiar with or to suit your faith, say "JE-SU" or "BUD-DHO".

Once seated comfortably, say a prayer inviting the divine to provide you with guidance. The Gayatri Mantra is a suitable mantra that can be chanted three times before commencing any meditation.

Breathe evenly with the sound of the "SO-HUM" mantra, as mentioned above. Close the eyes and imagine that there is a light in front of you and keep visualising this light for a few moments. Using your imagination, bring this light to the forehead, between the two eye brows, and slowly move this light into your head and fill the whole head with this light. Once the light fills your head, think the thought below:

"Wherever there is light, darkness cannot be present and I will only have good thoughts."

Those of us who are unable to visualise the light could gaze at the flame of a lamp or candle for a few minutes and then close the eyes and then try and concentrate on this light.

Now move the light to the eyes and fill them with this divine glow and think:

Let me see good in all things.

Then move the light to the ears and fill both ears with it and think,

Let me hear only good things.

From the ears, slowly move the light to your mouth and tongue and think:

Let me speak the truth, what is useful, necessary, and speak kindly to everyone.

From the mouth move the light along the neck, shoulders and arms, illuminating every cell on the way to the hands. Fill both hands with this light and think:

Let me do only good things and serve all.

Then move the light up the arms and down the torso to the feet, illuminating every cell of the limbs along the way. Now think:

Let me walk straight to the destination and to good places, and only meet and associate with good people.

Now bring the light up the legs, through the torso to the heart and then to the head and leave it here for a few minutes.

Then imagine that the light from your heart is radiating out and it is surrounding your mother and father. They are now standing in the divine light. Now think that they are in peace. Continue to extend this light radiating from your heart to cover your teachers, relatives, friends, and expand it further outside to cover all human beings, animals, birds, insects, plants and the whole world. Now think:

The world is filled with light, love and peace.

Remain immersed in this light and send it to every corner of the universe and think:

The light is in me... I AM THE LIGHT.

Continue to breathe evenly for a few moments, mentally chanting the sound "SO" when inhaling and "HUM" when exhaling. Then end the meditation with a prayer of gratitude to God. The prayer could be:

Samastah Lokah sukhino bhavantu (May the world be happy)

You can recite this three times.

14

YOGA

Yoga has been a part of the Hindu tradition since early Vedic period. The word Yoga comes from the Sanskrit root 'Yuj', which means union between one's personal consciousness and universal consciousness. Yoga is a means of enlightenment.

Karma Yoga, Bhakti Yoga, Jnana Yoga and Raja Yoga are considered as the four main types of yoga. **Karma Yoga** is a path based on selfless actions such as service to others with selfless devotion and without the thought of reward. Swami Vivekananda summaries Karma Yoga as follows:

> *"Give your hand to work and keep your mind fixed at the lotus feet of the lord. Do your duty, give up results, serve God or the self in all and follow the discipline."*

Bhakti Yoga is a path based on devotion and divine love. It is practiced through prayers, worship and rituals, while submitting to God. Chanting and singing also form a major part of the practice.

Raja Yoga is the comprehensive method of controlling the mind by turning our mental and physical energy into spiritual energy through meditation. Practicing the asanas and pranayama (breath control) form a subdivision of Raja Yoga known as the Hatha Yoga.

Jnana Yoga is a path based on knowledge and wisdom, and uses the mind to inquire into its own nature. The practice of Jnana Yoga requires strong willpower and intellect and the knowledge of other yogic paths.

In the modern world, yoga has come to be associated with postures (asanas) of Hatha Yoga. The aim of Hatha Yoga is to promote mental and physical health, and attain mastery over the body. This is achieved through proper diet, exercise, maintain the right posture, breathing correctly, practicing techniques to calm the mind and through meditation. Yoga encompasses more than the asanas and exercises practiced in the West. Hatha Yoga is a form of physical purification and training that prepares the aspirant for the higher practice called Raja Yoga.

15

KARMA

Major religions that originated in India — Hinduism, Buddhism, Jainism and Sikhism — all accept the universality of the law of cause and effect — karma.

In Sanskrit, 'Kar' stands for the organ of action and 'Ma' means producing or creating. Therefore 'Karma' refers to that which is created or produced by one's physical and mental organs. Karma is action driven by intention; a deed done deliberately by body and mind, speech included. In short, any work or action, physically or mentally, produces an effect called karma.

In the Upanishads, karma is expressed as a principle of cause and effect based on actions. It is regarded as a fundamental law of nature that is automatic and mechanical. That is, every action must have an effect either immediately or at some time in the future. It is not something imposed by God and it is not interfered with.

Hinduism believes that our karma determines what we deserve and what we can assimilate. We are responsible for what we have and we have the power to make our life.

In Hinduism, karma is the force of retributive justice that compels believers to behave righteously according to dharma, the moral code of the universe.

The concept of karma is deeply ingrained in the consciousness of Hindus and vastly influences their thinking. While a Hindu may not think of his karma while performing his daily duties, it is ingrained deep in his subconscious mind, influencing every action. Whether a follower is literate or illiterate, he honours it and accepts that he is responsible for the present condition of his life.

Sathya Sai Baba has said that the impending consequences of an action in innumerable past lives is an enormous karmic force. He also said that our present birth came about because of that karmic force and until we get free of the entangling the web of action and reaction our karmic destiny will continue through aeons of time, until eventually we do get free.

Karma also encourages good actions in Hindus, as they believe that bad karma could be counteracted by rightful actions. According to Baba, if one covers the seed sufficiently with soil then it does not geminate and grow. In the same way, if we cover our bad karma sufficiently with good actions then the effect of the bad karma will be dissolved.

It is also said in scriptures that the seeds of bad, sinful and harmful actions could be sufficiently covered by a number of good actions, such as pilgrimage to holy places, acts of devotion and performing loving service to others. Thus, bad karma gets burned away and do not grow into a new round of misery.

The *Bhagavad Gita*, chapter 4, verse 19 states:

> *"He whose undertakings are all devoid of desires and selfish purposes and whose actions have been burnt by the fire of knowledge, him the wise call a sage."*

The root cause of our suffering comes from desires and thus the scriptures caution us against actions that are motivated by desire. The scriptures further state that contact with the sense objects results in attachment. Attachment then becomes desire. From desire comes anger and out of anger comes delusion. Delusion leads to confusion of memory, which in turn leads to loss of intellect or discrimination. With the loss of intellect, man perishes. Therefore, it is important to perform our actions with good intentions and reason according to the context and devoid of selfish purpose.

By not performing an action one cannot avoid bad karma. For example, if we walk away from a person who is physically injured and needs help, then that could result in bad karma. Therefore, one should give sufficient thought to the context of the situation before deciding to act or not. Krishna explains this to Arjuna as follows in chapter 2, verse 33, of the *Gita*:

> *"But if thou will not fight this righteous war, then having abandoned thine own duty and fame, thou shalt incur sin."*

To keep the whole universe and its creation moving smoothly, everyone, including stones, plants and animals have a part to play. Thus, the whole universe is a workshop where everyone is allocated a task they have to perform. Whatever task is, it should be undertaken as an offering to God, that is, without any desire of benefitting from it. Even a wise person should be engaged in activity such that they serve as an example to others. There is no single item in this universe that is devoid of action. Everything contributes in some form or other. The main difference between humans and other things in the universe is that we are eager to reap the rewards of our actions whereas the plants and animals go on regardless, thus keeping the cycle of creation moving smoothly.

Sri Sathya Sai Baba has also said that as long as we perform actions in order to reap rewards, we are fully involved in and are a part and parcel of that process. Therefore, we must experience the consequences of the process, whether they are positive or not. When we remove our self from the throne of the doer and let God, the rightful king, take the throne, we are at once released from the burden of kingship.

Swami Vivekananda suggested, *"work for work's sake."* There are some, in every country, who are really the salt of the earth and work for the sake of work, without any care for reward, fame, name or even a ticket to heaven.

Krishna stresses on the above concept in the *Gita*, chapter 4, verse 23, as follows:

> *"To one who is devoid of attachment, who is liberated, whose mind is established in knowledge, who works for the sake of sacrifice (for the sake of God), the whole action is dissolved."*

Karma is summarised in the *Bhagavad Gita* as follows:

> *Your right is to work only,*
>
> *But never to its fruits,*
>
> *Let not the fruits of action be thy motive,*
>
> *Nor let thy attachment be to inaction.*

Karma should not be confused with fate. In the notion of fate, one's life is pre-planned by some external, divine power and has no control over the destiny. In the epic, the *Mahabharata*, there is extensive debate regarding free will and destiny across different chapters. It concludes that the future is both a function of current human effort derived from free will and past human actions that set the circumstances. The *Mahabharata* also states:

> *"Happiness comes due to good actions, suffering results in evil actions, by actions all things are obtained, by inaction, nothing whatsoever is enjoyed. If one's action bore no fruits, then everything is to no avail, if the world worked from fate alone, it would be neutralized."*

Although most Westerners, influenced by Christianity, do not believe in karma, there are a number of Western phrases that have similar meaning. For example: Violence begets violence; What goes around comes around; As you sow so shall you reap; Live by the sword, die by the sword and so on. The main difference between Hinduism and Christianity is that most people consider the concept of the Judgement Day as different from karma, because karma is an ongoing process that occurs on a daily basis and continues even after death. The Judgement Day in contrast is a onetime review at the end of one's life.

Karma is also associated with rebirth or reincarnation, in which a person is reborn after death in accordance with one's actions that are carried over from the present life. Therefore, the balance effect of one's actions can be revisited upon a person in his future life, too.

16
REINCARNATION (REBIRTH)

The concept of rebirth or reincarnation is accepted by all Indian spiritual traditions. This concept is familiar to most people. Although most people cannot remember their past lives, there are a few who can recollect their immediate past lives and are even able to recognise certain places and former relatives. It is said that Lord Buddha was able to remember several of his past lives.

In Hinduism, the Sanskrit word that closely resembles the soul is atma, which is the immortal essence hidden in every object created, including humans. That is, the God within us is called atma. Therefore, atma never dies, it is eternal, but takes a different body depending on the past actions or karma.

In the *Bhagavad Gita,* chapter 2, verse 20, defines atma as:

> *"It is not born, nor does it die; after having been, it again ceases not to be unborn, eternal, changeless and ancient. It is not killed when body is killed."*

One's karma gets imprinted and remains in that person's consciousness. Depending on the good and bad karma, the soul (atma) takes rebirth in higher or lower realms. This process of rebirth is a continuous cycle in which the soul is reborn over and over again, according to one's karma. This is called *Samsara.*

In the *Bhagavad Gita*, chapter 2, verse 27, it says:

> *"For certain is death for the born, and certain is birth for the dead; therefore, over the inevitable thou shouldst not grieve."*

The process of death and rebirth is similar to plants in the spring, forming new buds that grow into leaves and flowers in summer, and in autumn they change colours to yellow and orange and fall away. Then the plants become dormant in winter and the process starts all over again the following year. Similarly, the soul enters a new body from its season of infancy, youth and old age. When the body dies, the whole process start all over again.

In karma, there is an accounting system, that is, whenever we do a good deed or favour to others, we get credits and whenever we receive favours from others or do bad deeds, our points get debited. As we live our lives, we get so many credits and debits, and our next life will be decided depending on our balance points.

Hindus believe there is no eternal heaven or hell, and that no person will be denied the oneness with God — enlightenment (moksha). It is a matter of time for the karma to work its way through to attain enlightenment. In each birth, one learns lessons, which will help to progress in the cycle of rebirth to the goal of liberation (moksha). This progressive evolution carries each soul (atma) through a long evolutionary journey until it finally merges with the universal consciousness. This life journey continues for several eons from stone to plant, plant to animal, animal to human, to super human and to the divine.

17

HINDUISM AND SCIENCE

17.1 The Hindu View of Science

Hinduism is based on the foundation of science and freedom of thought. It never persecuted scientists like in the Western world, where scientists were victimized in the name of religion. For example, Italian scientist and physicist Galileo (1564-1620) was convicted in 1633 for publishing his evidence supporting the Copernican theory that the Earth revolved around the Sun, which was contrary to the belief of the Roman Catholic Church that the Sun revolved around the Earth.

Hinduism never discouraged or prevented scientific thoughts, and instead, it incorporated science into the religion. The Hindu faith was never allowed to run counter to scientific laws.

Veda is the body of knowledge that formed the foundation of Hinduism. In addition to the four main Vedas (referred to in Section 1), Vedic literature also contains such works as Ayurveda (the science of holistic medicine), *Dhanurveda* (the military science), *Gandhara* Veda (the art of music, dance, etc.), *Arta-sastkam* (science of government), etc.

17.2 Mathematics and Hinduism

The Vedas also contain mathematics, which was essential for the calculation of movements related to the solar system that was used to predict the religious festivals. In fact, the number system used by the Indians was passed to the Middle East and was being used by the Arabs since 700 AD. This was then passed to Europe and they called it the Arabic numbers. The change in the number system from the Roman numbers to the Indian Hindu numbers (referred to as Arabic numbers by the West) enabled the development of mathematics and science in Europe as we know it today.

The significance of the development of the number system was described by the French mathematician Pierre Simon Laplace (1749-1827) as follows:

> *"It is India that gave us the ingenious method of expressing all numbers by the means of ten symbols, each symbol receiving a value of position, as well as an absolute value; a profound and important idea which appears so simple to us now that we ignore its true merit, but its very simplicity, the great ease which it has lent to all computations, puts our arithmetic in the first rank of useful inventions, and we shall appreciate the grandeur of this achievement when we remember that it escaped the genius of Archimedes and Apollonius, two of the greatest minds produced by antiquity."*

(Quoted in *Return to Mathematical Circles*, H. Eves, Boston 1988)

Professor Edward Lorentz, mathematician, meteorologist and the father of Chaos Theory, noticed that a tiny difference in initial parameters in a complex weather system would result in a completely different behaviour. This is the reason why scientists are finding it very difficult to predict the weather accurately. Nature is a highly complex system and the only prediction one can make is that she is unpredictable.

Kurt Gödel, a mathematician, proposed the Incompleteness Theorem, which states that no axiomatic system can ever prove the consistency of its own axioms and therefore remains incomplete. He also stated that no logical system will ever be able to prove everything and Truth cannot be reached by logic, Truth is singular, Truth is one, God.

Hinduism teaches that one can only experience God, the Truth, and not find it by logical reasoning. In the *Gita*, chapter 12, verses 08, 09, 10 & 11, Krishna states the method by which one could experience God.

In verse 08, the yoga of meditation and contemplation is prescribed for advance students.

In verse 09, the yoga of constant practice of spiritual discipline is prescribed, such as rituals or deity worship.

If the above are difficult, verse 10 prescribes doing one's duty towards God without any selfish motive. If one cannot do any of the above, then in verse 11, it says,

> *"Resorting to union with Me, renounce the fruits of all actions, at the same time practicing self–control. This is the easiest path of all paths."*

17.3 Cosmology and Hinduism

Hinduism is dedicated to the idea of the cosmos.

The cosmos undergoes an immense number of cycles of repeated birth and death, from day and night to day and night of Brahma, which is 8.64 billion years. This time scale corresponds to those of the modern scientific thinking of the cosmos.

The duration of day and night of Brahma is stated in the *Bhagavad Gita*, chapter 8, verse 17, as follows:

> *"Those who know Brahma's day which comprises the duration of four billion three hundred and twenty million years and His night also the duration of four billion and three hundred and twenty million years are knowers of day and night."*

The cycle of birth and rebirth is also stated in the *Gita*, chapter 8, verse 16, as follows:

> *"The resident of all the worlds, O Arjuna, from Brahma's world the most evolved material planet in all the trillions of universes, downwards are subjected to the cycle of repeated birth and death; but by taking refuge in Me, O Arjuna, repeated birth ceases."*

The elegant representation of the creation of the universe at a cosmic cycle is a *murti*, known as the cosmic dance of Lord Siva, *Natarajah*, (*Nata*= dance, *raja*= king, the king of dance).

The dance is interpreted as the source of all movements in the universe, the origin of the free cosmic powers, and his gracious action in liberating the souls.

Natarajah

In the form of Natarajah, Lord Siva carries his *damaru* (drum) and *agni* (flame) in his upper hands . The sound of the *damaru* represents the sound of creation and removal of impurities or maya.

Agni is a reminder that the newly-created universe will be utterly destroyed in billions of years and it will burn all karma.

The lower right-hand makes *abhayamudra* (a gesture that allays fears).

The front-hand pointing to the raised left foot signifies refuge of the troubled souls.

The dwarf-like figure, demon, trampled by Siva's right foot represents illusion (or ignorance).

The whirling of the hair depicts the dynamic of the dance.

Here it's of interest to observe that modern physics has also revealed that every subatomic particle is also in an energy dance state, in a pulsating process of creation and destruction.

17.4 The Significance of the Number 108 in Hinduism

The number **108** is very auspicious in Hindu cosmology. It is the number of beads in the rosary used in meditation. The ancient Indian took this number, 108, to be the distance between the Sun and the Earth in Sun-diameter units. The distance between the Sun and the Earth, divided by the Sun's diameter, is equal to 108 (149,597,870,700km/1,392,000 km= 108).

According to Ayurveda, the 107 *marmas* (weak spots) in the body is held by a chain of 108 "links". In the inner cosmology of the human body, the number 108 is also taken to represent the "distance" between the body of the devotee to God within. This is the reason why we do our mantras 108 times, using the rosary with 108 beads, as it is a symbol of our spiritual journey towards our higher self (the Sun) from our material self (the Earth).

17.5 Hinduism and Quantum Physics

The resident classical theory of science proposed from the time of Isaac Newton up to the mid-twenties provided a model of the world made of objects in a predictable way. These classical theories by scientists like Newton, James Clerk Maxwell, Thomas Young, James Prescott Joule, John Dalton and others dealt with mechanics, electricity, heat, optics and so on, which are extensively used in engineering and technology even today. In these theories that are very familiar to us, matter is assumed to be a large aggregate of many particles, existing at a specific time and specific place, obeying the laws of motion, conservation of energy and so on. In this classical regime of science, the quantum fluctuations are sufficiently small that they can be ignored, as envisaged by the Newtonian framework, and the atomic and subatomic effects were not accommodated in the classical framework.

By the beginning of the 20th century, experimental data and inconsistency in the classical scientific theories, due to the inability to accommodate the atomic sub atomic effects, compelled physicists to accept the two revolutionary concepts of Quantum Theory and Relativity Theory. Scientists discovered that atomic and subatomic particles are discrete packets of energy. These individual units are called *quanta* (Latin for 'how much'). French physicist Louis de Broglie proposed that matter and energy at the atomic and subatomic level may behave either as if made of wave-like and particle-like properties. These ideas led to the branch of physics called quantum mechanics.

In the theory of quantum mechanics, the subatomic particles that form the protons are called quarks and gluons. Quarks have up and down charges and are held together by gluons, as shown.

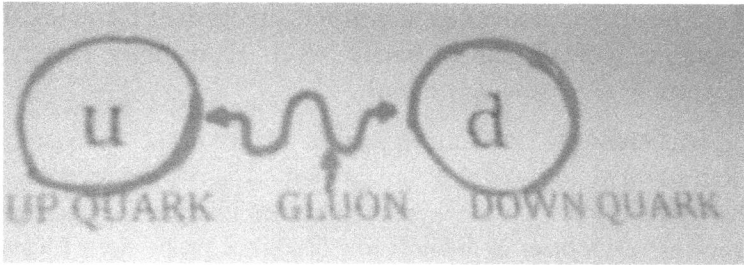

UP QUARK   GLUON   DOWN QUARK

Electrons surround the nucleus in a form of a cloud, as electrons can occupy fixed, but different, orbits. An electromagnetic force holds the electrons and the tiny nucleus together.

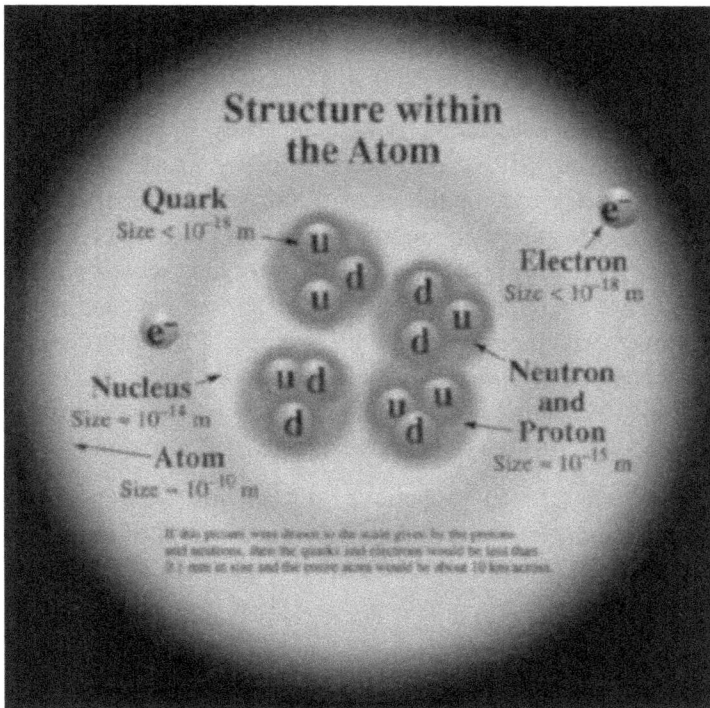

Structure within the Atom

Quark
Size < 10^{-18} m

Electron
Size < 10^{-18} m

Nucleus
Size ~ 10^{-14} m

Atom
Size ~ 10^{-10} m

Neutron and Proton
Size ~ 10^{-15} m

The current understanding of the structure of the atom, the quantum view, is shown above, (Ref: Elementary Particles, Lecture, University of Oregon).

According to quantum physicists, matter in the universe has both *particle and wave like properties.* It is not that everything behaves at times like a wave and at times like particles and visa versa. Every object in the universe has some properties of waves and some of particles, but it is not either. This new kind of particles are referred to as *quantum particles* and behave like matter with energy distributed in discrete, countable chunks. That is, energy is not smooth and continuous as assumed in classical science but comes in a specific fixed amount, just like the hand of a clock that *ticks* from number to number. This idea that some properties of objects *ticked* like a dial with a specific setting is called *quantized.* Albert Einstein's theory showed that it is not only energy but electromagnetic radiation itself was quantized in this manner.

Albert Einstein along with colleagues Boris Podolsk and Nathan Rosen (EPR) published a paper in 1935, showing mathematically that in the atomic and subatomic level, under certain circumstances, quantum mechanics predicted breakdown of locality. *Locality* is the principle that an event, which happens at one place, cannot instantaneously affect an event at another place. The paper, which predicted the breakdown of locality, concluded that if one puts a particle in a measuring device at one location, by simply by doing this, it instantly influenced another particle far away. Today, this theory is known as the EPR Paradox.

Einstein refused to believe this as this went against his Special Theory of Relativity, where the concept of locality was necessary for him to predict that no signal could travel faster than light.

In the meantime, Werner Heisenberg, a German theoretical physicist and one of the key pioneers of quantum mechanics, proposed that the precise and simultaneous measurement of two complementary values, the position and momentum of subatomic particles, is impossible. For example, if the position of an electron is measured, its momentum cannot be measured and any attempt to measure it will be flawed. This theory is known as the Uncertainty Principle. This prompted Albert Einstein to make his famous comment:

"God does not play dice."

To this, Niels Bohr, a Danish physicist and Nobel laureate who was working on the quantized model of atom, replied,

"Not to tell God what to do."

Thirty years later, in 1965, John Stewart Bell, the originator of Bell's Theorem, resolved this EPR Paradox by proving mathematically that the results predicated by quantum mechanics could not be explained — which preserved locality. This is called the Bell's Theorem. This theorem established that the world is non-local. Locality means no instantaneous (spooky) action at a distance. That is, a physical process occurring at one place should not have any immediate effect on the particle at another location.

This lead to one of the strangest and most important consequences of quantum mechanics—the idea of "entanglement" — when two particles from the same source interact in a certain way, their state will depend on one another, even if they are separated. For example, if you hold one particle in Sydney and another in Colombo and measure them simultaneously, the outcome of the result in Sydney will determine the outcome of the result in Colombo and visa versa. This was proved in 1972 by experiments conducted by Professor John Clauser at Berkley, confirming Bell's Theorem. The experiments have shown that two or more electrons or protons demonstrated correlated properties even at a great distance, where no communication is possible between them, during a given time. That is, the particles can talk to each other faster than light. Bell's Theorem and associated implications regarding the nature of the physical world remains of great interest and research to this day. Although it has been proved mathematically and experimentally, it still remains a controversy.

The above scientific theory has forced scientists to consider the idea that a pure objective world is in conflict with the theory of quantum mechanics which reveals a profound interaction between conscious mental activity and the physical world. Although this has been proven by mathematical theory and experimentation, our logical mind, conditioned by the classical scientific theories, has great difficulty comprehending this new finding. Scientists consider this discovery in quantum mechanics as one of the most important discoveries in science.

In modern physics, the idea of the connection with consciousness has been associated with the observation of the atomic phenomena described above. In these phenomena, quantum physics has made it clear that this can only be understood as a link in a chain process, the end of which lies in the consciousness of the human observer.

In this way, scientists are becoming increasingly aware of the essential unity in all things and events.

The *Bhagavad Gita*, chapter 13, verses 15 & 16 says:

> *"And undivided, yet It exists as if divided in beings; It is known as the supporter of beings; It devours and It generates.*
>
> *Within and without all living entities, ultimate truth is stationary as well as mobile; an account of its being subatomic, that ultimate truth is incomprehensible and is far away yet also very near."*

Nick Herbert, an American physicist and author best known for his book *Quantum Reality*, suggests that we have merely discovered the oneness that the physical world and consciousness cannot be regarded as separate entities. He has also stated that appearance is what we see and everything around us. Reality is the secret behind things. There is a connection between them, and it is at the level of reality and not at the level of appearance. This underground connection can be proven but not seen.

Quantum physicists now say that each part of the universe contains all the information present in the entire cosmos itself, just like the very small seed of the banyan tree contains all the information to replicate itself.

In Hinduism, consciousness is Brahman who is present in everything. Hinduism constantly refers to the awareness of unity and mutual interaction of all things and events, just like the quantum particles affecting each other even though separated by vast distances. This ultimate reality, which manifests in all things where all things are parts, is called Brahman.

Hinduism arrived at the same conclusions starting from the inner realm, whereas scientists have arrived at it from the external world.

As scientists go deeper and deeper with these new theories, they keep finding that there is a fuzzy world underlying matter and material objects.

Niels Bohr proposed that a particle is whatever it is measured to be, wave or particle, but cannot be assumed to have specific properties or even to exist until it is measured. If a scientist looks for a particle using a particle detector, then he finds a particle, but if the scientist looks for a wave and uses a wave detector, then he finds a wave pattern. In short, Bohr was saying that objective reality does not exist. As the underlying nature of the whole universe is becoming fuzzier, it appears as an illusion to the scientists.

In Hinduism, the concept of maya explains this kind of illusion. Maya refers to that which is not — an illusion. According to Hinduism, Maya is a web of deception weaved by the universal spider, Brahman, to envelop the world in delusion. The world is both real, because it exists, and unreal,

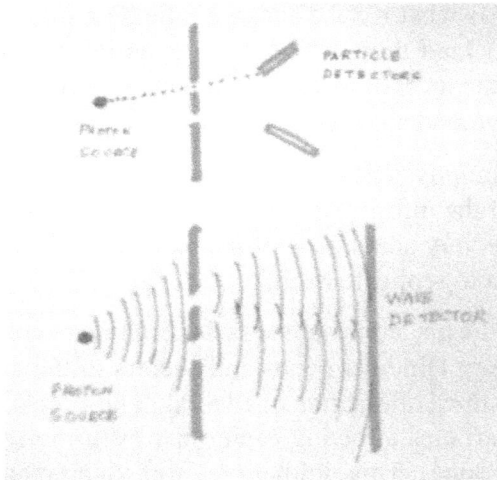

because it is not what it appears to be — just like the electron being a wave or a particle.

Hinduism considers the universe to be unreal in an absolute and eternal sense. The material universe is a temporary creation and keeps changing constantly never staying the same. It is an illusion because it conceals the truth and reveals itself differently each time we perceive it.

Physical science started by explaining the mysteries of the external world, but at the farthest end of this research – the subatomic level, it finds itself face to face with the mystery of man, mind and consciousness.

Hinduism constantly refers to unity and the mutual interaction of all things and events. This ultimate reality is called Brahman, the one who pervades all things. This basic oneness is not only the central theme of Hinduism but also an important revolution in modern physics, which becomes apparent at the atomic level when scientists delve into the realm of subatomic particles.

Science has no conflict with Hinduism or religion in general. Both have the identical aim of discovering the truth and helping humans to achieve their full potential. But each by itself has only been partially successful. While the older Eastern civilization took guidance from the scriptures of Hinduism and other religions that followed, modern Western civilization took guidance from science.

The achievement of both civilizations in creating a harmonious, peaceful world has been limited. Regardless, scientists starting from the external world and Hinduism starting from the inner realm have arrived at the same conclusion of basic oneness of the universe.

The combination of the two disciplines — science and religion — in the life of a human being will help him to grow physically, mentally and spiritually, and thus building a more complete society.

Swami Vivekananda lucidly expressed the above as follows:

"Each soul is potentially divine. The goal is to manifest this Divinity within, by controlling nature, external and internal. Do this either by work, or worship, or psychic control, or philosophy — by one or more or all of these — and be free. This is the whole of religion. Doctrines, or dogmas, or rituals, or books, or temples, or forms, are but secondary details."

Ancient Hindu thinkers and rishis did not talk about religion and science as we do now. They categorised knowledge into two — *Apara Vidya* (material knowledge) and *Para Vidya* (spiritual knowledge). One is incomplete without the other.

Appendix A
The Grantha Script

கூ	வ	ழ	வ	ஐ
k	kh	g	gh	ṅ

உ	உ	ஜ	ஙூ	ஞ
c	ch	j	jh	ñ

ட	౦	உ	உ	ண
ṭ	ṭh	ḍ	ḍh	ṇ

த	ழு	உ	ய	ந
t	th	d	dh	n

ப	பெ	ப	ழ	உ
p	ph	b	bh	m

ய	ா	௨	வ	௨
y	r	l	v	ḷ

ா	ஷ	வ	ஹ	
ś	ṣ	s	h	

அ அா இ ஈ உ ஊ
a ā i ī u ū

஌ ௠ எ ஏ
ṛ ṝ ḷ ḹ

எ ஏ ஒ ஔ
e ai o au

◦ ◦◦
ṃ ḥ

REFERENCES

1. Bhalla, P. P. *HINDU Rites, Rituals, Customs & Traditions.* (2009).

2. BHAGAVAD GITA TRUT. *Bhagavad Gita.* (1988-2015) USA.

3. Einstein, Albert and Plank, Max. *Quantum Mechanics for Beginners.*

4. Einstein, Albert; Podolsky, Boris; Rosan, Nathan. *Can Quantum-Mechanical Description of Physical Reality Be Considered Complete?* (1935).

5. Gangaahar B N et al. *Neurohemodynamic correlates of OM Chanting, A pilot functional magnetic resonance Imaging Study. International Journal of Yoga Jan- Jun 2011*

6. Gurjar Ajay Anil, Ladhake S A, Ehakare A P. *Analysis of Acoustic of OM Chant to Study it's Effect on Nervous System. International Journal of Computer Science and Network Security Vol 9 No1 2009.*

7. Haddad, Ella H; Sabate, Joan; Whitten, Crystal. *Vegetarian food guide pyramid.* (1999).

8. Hislop, S. John. *MY BABA and I.*

9. HUMAN VALUES EDUCATION FOR THE NEW AGE. Bangkok, Thailand. (1987).

10. Krishnaswami, K. R. *Agamas (Indian Tradition of Image Worship).*

11. Lakkani, Jay. Head of Hindu Academy of Education. Director for the Hindu Council UK and a Theoretical Physicist. *Advanced Hinduism.* (2013).

12. Lakshminarasimha B. Puranic K. H. Rangarajan H. *Agamas Susama.* (2005).

13. Maheshwari Gavri (Danielle Riordan). *Basics of Hinduism,* Karan digital media.

14. Milton R Mills MD. The Comparative Anatomy of Eating. Vegsource 2009.

15. Shivam Joshi MD , Physician . Think we evolved to eat meat? Think again. Huffington Post

16. Sivananda, Sri Swami. *THE BHAGAVAD GITA.* (1982).

17. Sutton, N. Professor at Oxford Centre of Hindu Studies, Continuing Education Department. (Ref www.ochs.org.uk/ced). *Talks on Hindu Religious Philosophy.* (2008-2013).

18. University of Oregon. Elementary particles.

19. Wikipedia

About the Author

Kandiah Sivaloganathan hails from a traditional Hindu family from the village of Suthumali, Jaffna, Sri Lanka.

He completed his early education in Sri Lanka, at Manipay Hindu College, Jaffna, and at St Benedict's College, Colombo.

He graduated in Engineering with honours from the University of Ceylon, Sri Lanka.

Thereafter, Mr. Sivaloganathan obtained his Master's degree in Engineering from the University of New South Wales, Sydney, Australia.

He is a member of the Institution of Engineers, London, UK, Hong Kong and Australia.

Mr. Sivaloganathan has travelled extensively and has worked both as an engineer and a consultant in Sri Lanka, United Kingdom, Hong Kong and Australia.

He had showed a keen interest in spirituality from his early years itself and has devoted his life to spiritual pursuits ever since.

He is a devotee of Bhagawan Sri Sathya Sai Baba and has been involved with the Sathya Sai Movement for more than 35 years.

He was also an active member of the Sathya Sai Centre of Hong Kong.

He and his family were fortunate to have interviews with Bhagawan Sri Sathya Sai Baba in 1988.